The Battle of

5–7 February

Steve Watt

Steve Watt has been researching the Anglo-Boer War for over 35 years. His work has resulted in a seminal publication of the deaths and graves of the Imperial forces engaged in the conflict. He has conducted numerous tours around the battle sites, published many articles and presented papers at conferences on his specific field of interest.

The Anglo-Boer War Battle Series:

The Battle of Talana: 20 October 1899 (978-1-928211-39-6)

The Battle of Elandslaagte: 21 October 1899 (978-1-928211-40-2)

The Battle of Modder Spruit and Tchrengula: The Fight for Ladysmith, 30 October 1899 (978-1-928211-48-8)

The Battle of Colenso: 15 December 1899 (978-1-928211-41-9)

The Battle of Spioenkop: 23–24 January 1900 (978-1-928211-42-6)

The Battle of Vaalkrans: 5–7 February 1900 (978-1-928211-43-3)

The Siege of Ladysmith: 2 November 1899–28 February 1900 (978-1-928211-44-0)

The Relief of Ladysmith: Breakthrough at Thukela Heights: 13–28 February 1900 (978-1-928211-45-7)

A Guide to the Anglo-Boer War Sites of KwaZulu-Natal (978-1-928211-46-4)

The Anglo-Boer War Sites of KwaZulu-Natal: boxed set of 9 titles (978-1-928211-52-5)

First published in 1999 by Ravan Press

This edition published in 2014 by:
30° South Publishers (Pty) Ltd
16 Ivy Road
Pinetown 3610
South Africa
info@30degreessouth.co.za
www.30degreessouth.co.za

ISBN 978-1-928211-43-3

Designed & typeset by Blair Couper
Cover design by Kerrin Cocks
Cartography by Toni Bodington & Olive Anderson, Cartographic Unit, University of Natal (Pietermaritzburg) & Phil Wright
Photographs & sketches courtesy of the Talana Museum, Ken Gillings and the author
Printed by Pinetown Printers, Durban, South Africa

Contents

Preface

This Battle Book series has been written to make information, photographs and maps of the most significant Anglo-Boer War sites in KwaZulu-Natal more readily available.

The books are not exhaustive studies of the various sites but rather field guides, designed to assist the reader in interpreting the terrain and understanding the events.

Although the Battle Books form a series, each book has been fully contextualized and can be followed on its own.

Contributors to this series share a long-term interest in the Anglo-Boer War and have each made their own unique contribution to the historiography and understanding of the conflict. With the assistance of an editorial committee, every effort has been made to maintain balance and accuracy.

A slightly flexible approach has been adopted to the spelling of names. As a general rule, the most recent spelling utilized on the state's Survey and Mapping 1:50 000 maps has been adopted. Thus for instance Laing's Nek becomes Lang's Nek. Where the name used to describe a topographical feature differs significantly from that in the historical literature to that appearing on the map, then the one used in the books and documents is adopted. The spelling of the river Thukela (Tugela) presents a slight problem. On maps it is spelt as given in the brackets. However, in most current academic historical literature the former form has been adopted, which spelling has been followed in this series of books.

Background

On 11 October 1899 the Anglo-Boer War began with the Boer invasion of the Natal and Cape Colonies. Nowhere, from a Boer point of view, did the situation call more urgently for immediate action than on the Natal border. Both the Transvaal commandos and those from the Orange Free State invaded Natal via passes in the Drakensberg.

It was obvious to the Natal government that the Boers were planning to encircle the British forces north of the Thukela River. Major-General Penn Symons, with a force concentrated at Dundee, declined to retire to Ladysmith, where a larger force under Lieutenant-General Sir George White, VC, had gathered. Symons had hoped that he could confidently hold Dundee against enemy attack.

The Boers attacked Dundee from Talana Hill (20 October 1899) and, although they were repulsed, Major-General JH Yule, on whom devolved the command (Symons being mortally wounded), decided to withdraw the British force to Ladysmith. In an effort to restore railway communication with Dundee, White attacked the Boers at Elandslaagte (21 October 1899) to drive them off. After receiving the news about the Boer reverse, the Free State commandos were ordered to Elandslaagte. There followed the engagement at Rietfontein (24 October 1899). This was an inconclusive event with neither side claiming victory. The Boers began gathering in large numbers around Ladysmith. In an effort to drive off the Boers, White's force attacked them at Tchrengula and Modderspruit (30 October 1899). The British force was unsuccessful and forced to retire into Ladysmith, leaving the Boers to complete the investment (siege) of the town.

In early November a Boer council of war decided to send a strong reconnaissance party southwards to ascertain the strength and positions of British reinforcements which had entered Natal. There followed a skirmish near Frere, during which an armoured train was ambushed (15 November 1899) and Winston Churchill, then a British war correspondent, was captured.

Elated by their success the Boers advanced on Estcourt and, with the intention of barring any British reinforcements from the town, occupied the high ground to the south. There followed the engagement near Willow Grange (23 November 1899), during which the British were forced to retire on Estcourt. However, this action brought home to Commandant-General Piet Joubert that his force was too small in number to advance further into southern Natal. It was therefore decided to retire to the Thukela River at Colenso, to occupy the hills that lay just to the north. The Boers arrived there in late November.

General Redvers Buller VC was appointed by the War Office to command the British troops in South Africa. Both the Cape and Natal Colonies had been invaded by the Boers who besieged the towns of Kimberley, Mafikeng and Ladysmith. The British commander realized that the bulk of the enemy's strength was in Natal and that the relief of Ladysmith was all important.

Accordingly, Lord Methuen was entrusted with the relief of Kimberley, while Buller went to Natal, arriving at Frere in early December 1899.

Buller's task was to relieve Ladysmith. However, his first effort at Colenso on 15 December 1899 to break through the Boer positions along the Thukela ended in defeat. General Louis Botha's men, skillfully positioned, together with carefully masked artillery, were able to inflict a heavy loss on Buller's men. The British Natal Field Force, as it came to be called, retired to Frere to await reinforcements.

Once the reinforcements arrived, Buller's force marched westward to the upper Thukela. Lieutenant-General Sir Charles Warren, Buller's second-in-command, was to command the next attempt to relieve Ladysmith. The Boers, who observed the British movements, consolidated their positions on the heights westward to Spioenkop and iNtabamnyama. The British crossed the Thukela River and for four days tried to pierce the Boer defence line with frontal attacks on iNtabamnyama (20-23 January 1900) and little headway was made. Part of Warren's force then occupied Spioenkop. There followed a hard fought and costly battle for the control of the hill (24 January 1900). When darkness came both sides withdrew from the summit. Early the next morning the Boers discovered that the British had abandoned the hill, and re-occupied it without firing a shot. Not wanting to sustain further losses Buller ordered a withdrawal to the south of the Thukela. Another attempt to relieve Ladysmith had failed.

The plan to capture Vaalkrans

With the Ladysmith garrison weakening daily as a result of bombardment, inadequate food supplies and disease, Buller resolved once more to make an attempt to reach the beleaguered town. Viewing the heights across the Thukela from Swartkop, he identified an area which offered some likelihood of success, namely Vaalkrans Hill.

Here the barrier of hills was at its narrowest, with open country lying beyond. Viewed from the right bank, where Buller was, the summit of Vaalkrans appeared practicable for occupation with artillery, which from that position would command the plain and the wagon routes to Ladysmith.

Between 27 January and 2 February 1900 further British reinforcements arrived, consisting of artillery, cavalry, and infantry reservists – a total of 2 400 men and eight guns – so that Buller's force stood once more at its original strength of 26 000 to 27 000 men.

Towards the end of January Buller visited every brigade in turn and addressed the troops, assuring them that he now had the key to Ladysmith and they would be there within a week. His troops, whose confidence he had never lost, were as optimistic as himself and in the best of spirits. The week's rest, coupled with Buller's assurance, had produced a great recuperative effect upon the force, both physically and in terms of morale.

The steep hill of Swartkop was selected for the emplacement of artillery. In pursuit of this scheme a hot air balloon was attached to a wire cable to enable an observer to determine a route to its summit. Preparations for the construction of a road, 25 kilometres long, through rough country began on 27 January. It involved heavy work at Swartkop, up whose slope a slide was smoothed for the haulage of artillery. Especially difficult was the route over the nek between Naval Hill and Swartkop where treble teams of oxen (48 animals) hauled the guns to the southern slope hidden from view of the Boers. Furthermore, stormy weather hampered the construction teams. By 2 February 14 guns (six Naval 12-pr, two 15-pr field guns and six of a mountain battery) stood concealed amongst the trees on the top of Swartkop. Two 5-inch army guns, which it had been found impossible to drag up the steep slope, occupied a position immediately to the west of Swartkop. A 4.7-inch gun was emplaced on Naval Hill, while another was positioned on Mount Alice. In addition, two Naval 12-pr guns stood on a plateau north of Mount Alice. The remaining guns were, at this stage, with the infantry. Against these the Boers were estimated to have seven artillery pieces.

The observation ballon used by the British on the upper Thukela. The height of the hills rendered the balloon largely ineffective. Balloons were in use from 1885 in the British army.

On 3 February Buller issued orders for the planned attack. Vaalkrans, presumed to be at the extreme left-end of the Boer position, was the object of the assault. Three infantry brigades were detailed to capture it. To lure the Boers from the real point of the attack, a feint was arranged against Brakfontein by the 11th Infantry Brigade, supported by seven batteries of artillery (42 guns) commanded by Major General AS Wynne, who had replaced the wounded Major-General Woodgate. The fire from the naval guns on and under Mount Alice was also to cover the feint attack. During the attack the 4th Brigade supported by the 2nd Division were to take up a suitable position in preparation for the assault near

Between 27 January and 3 February a rough road was constructed from Mt Alice to Swartkop. Visible here is the final ascent, up a 40 degree incline onto Swartkop. To drag guns onto the summit a wire hawser was attached around them and fifty men then hauled them up. By the time the first two guns reached the summit the men had cut hands and were exhausted.

the pontoon bridge No.2 (map on page 39). It was hoped that when the Boers had been drawn to the apparently threatened position, another pontoon bridge would be assembled across the river, eastward of No.2 pontoon. Thereupon the batteries on Swartkop would shell Vaalkrans, to be joined by the field batteries moving across the river from their attack on Brakfontein. Vaalkrans was then to be assaulted and occupied by the infantry in order that artillery might be placed on the hill. Once the artillery

Tobias Smuts (1861–1916) Combat-General (Veggeneraal) commanded some of the Boer forces in the Vaalkrans area. He was a member of the First Volksraad of the Zuid-Afrikaanschse Republiek (Transvaal). He had fought in several wars against African people. He is shown with a Krag-Jorgensen rifle of which approximately only 100 were officially imported.

was on Vaalkrans it was to shell Brakfontein. Then the cavalry would pass Vaalkrans to the open ground beyond taking with them the Royal Horse Artillery battery.

The Boers were aware of the British presence on the upper Thukela. By the evening of Sunday 4 February a Boer force of some 3 600 men and ten guns was entrenched along a front of 20 kilometres from Doringkloof in the east to iNtabamnyama in the west. The defence of the eastern flank was entrusted to Combat-General Tobias Smuts.

The Boer centre, on the Brakfontein Heights, consisted of the Free Staters under Chief Commandant Marthinus Prinsloo, who was in overall command of the Boer force. General Schalk Burger commanded the western flank from a three-peaked hill called Drielingkoppe (known as Twin Peaks by the British as only two elevations were visible to them) to iNtabamnyama. Louis Botha was away in Pretoria and Johannesburg, attending to personal matters.

Preliminary moves and feint

By the night of 4 February the British had carried out their preliminary movements; the 11th Brigade had taken up positions on the Maconochie Koppies (also known collectively as One Tree Hill) behind which seven batteries of artillery had gathered in readiness. The remaining infantry brigades, detailed for the real attack, moved into bivouacs near the foot of Mount Alice and Naval Gun Hill.

The Boers observing the British movements, began to suspect a new attack. Their patrols reported the British massing behind the Maconochie Koppies and in front of Mount Alice and Naval Hill. Botha, and Lucas Meyer at Colenso, were informed of these developments and were asked to render assistance, Botha being urgently requested to return to the front.

At 06:00 on 5 February 1900 the 11th Infantry Brigade emerged from the Maconochie Koppies with two battalions in front, a third in support,

Brakfontein Heights as seen from the British side in 1900. The Free State commandos held these during the battle of Vaalkrans.

while the fourth held the bridgehead at the No.1 pontoon in the rear. Six field batteries came into action behind them, supported by a howitzer battery at the Koppies. The approximately 900 Free Staters, along whose front the bombardment was directed, had received instructions not to fire on the advancing troops until they were 400 metres from their position. When the British troops were within 1 500 metres of the enemy's position "the order was given to lie down and do nothing, and [on] no account to fire unless at a good target. We waited for three hours lying in the grass while our guns bombarded the hill before us". Shortly before noon five Boer guns, in position from Drielingkoppe to Brakfontein, began to shell the British batteries, and continued the bombardment for the next hour and a half. The feint attack having done all that it was intended to do, the word was given for the infantrymen to retire. As the men rose and turned about, the Boer musketry from Brakfontein burst into life with an immense discharge of rifles. Lieutenant Blake Knox, who was a medical officer with the Natal Field Force observed: "So sudden and so furious was this outburst of shot and shell that the whole plain was obscured by smoke and dust." The infantry regained the shelter of the Maconochie Koppies with a loss of one man killed and 27 wounded (two of whom died). Knox records with reference to a burial behind the Koppies: "Even the burials were not without their danger, as the enemy kept shelling us from Spion Kop, to the full view of which we were exposed throughout the service..." By then the pontoon No.2 recently assembled, offered a passage for the batteries to take up their positions close to Vaalkrans (see map Vaalkrans: 5 February 1900 on page 39).

Capture of Vaalkrans

Meanwhile preparations for the offensive on the British right flank went ahead. Setting out at 07:00, Major-General Hildyard's 2nd Brigade, Major-

General Lyttlton's 4th Brigade and Major-General Hart's 5th Brigade filed from their bivouacs under Mount Alice and Naval Gun Hill and halted near the foot of Swartkop. By mid-morning the 5-inch guns, and a little later the guns on Swartkop, unmasked and opened up an intense bombardment on Vaalkrans. Soon the batteries from the feint attack began arriving across the Thukela at a position south-west of Vaalkrans. The appearance of the batteries was the signal for the Royal Engineers to begin assembling No.3 pontoon, 1 350 metres south of Munger's Drift. A

Major-General Sir Neville Lyttelton (1845–1931) came to South Africa having served in the British army for 35 years. He was sent to Natal in command of the 4th Infantry Brigade.

Maxim Nordenfeldt gun (called Pom-Pom by the British) positioned on Vaalkrans, and snipping by the Johannesburg Commando 600 metres to the east, as well as the hills beyond, greatly disrupted the construction effort. However, the pontoon, 65 metres in length, was completed in 50 minutes with minimal loss. The attacking columns were ready, but it was another hour before the artillery from the feint attack came across the river. On their arrival on the plain between Swartkop and Vaalkrans, these guns and those on Swartkop itself, now 72 in all, concentrated their fire upon Vaalkrans. The hill was scarcely visible through the flames and the eruptions of exploding shells. Its garrison, 95 men of the Johannesburg Commando with a Pom-Pom, under the command of Commandant Ben Viljoen, suffered severely. The remainder of the commando, 300 to 400

Then: British artillery on the fringes of Swartkop. There are two guns of the Mountain Battery (on the left), a field gun Royal Field Artillery (centre) and a naval gun in the distance (right). Prior to the firing commencing the trees were partially sawn through and stayed with ropes. They were felled just prior to the firing commencing.

men, occupied positions east of Vaalkrans extending to Doringkloof. A lyddite shell burst near Viljoen,who was temporarily stunned, and four men near him were killed.

At 14:00 two battalions of Lyttelton's 4th Brigade, namely the 1st Durham Light Infantry and the 1st Rifle Brigade, descended to the pontoon bridge No. 3 (see map on page 39). The crossing of the river was accomplished swiftly by small groups of soldiers. They came under fire from Boers in the mealie fields and dongas on the other side of the river. To avoid the flanking fire under which the infantry found themselves on leaving the bridge, the troops then moved in file along the river bed under cover of its steep banks. Emerging into the open and deploying eastwards the troops encountered a heavy frontal attack by Boers on Vaalkrans and on their right flank in the vicinity of the Doornkloof Stream. Near the river several infantrymen were killed including Major Johnson-Smyth. Once the troops emerged above the bank of the Thukela, the Boer gunners on Doringkloof, who had been shelling the British artillery on Swartkop, directed their fire at the infantrymen. In response the 4.7-inch gun on Naval Gun Hill and guns on Swartkop attempted to silence these guns, while the other 4.7-inch gun on Mount

Now: During a visit in 1990 to the Swartkop summit it proved difficult to identify the site where the photo on page 14 was taken owing to thick vegetation. A visitor to the site is seated on the same rock where a British soldier rested in 1900.

Alice and the two 5-inch guns diverted their attention to the targets on the Twin Peaks, Brakfontein and Vaalkrans. The Durham Light Infantry and Rifle Brigade, on broad fronts and in open formations, were able to begin their forward movement. At 16:00 both battalions reached the foot of Vaalkrans. After a pause the Durhams climbed Vaalkrans with bayonets fixed and at 16:30 drove off a few Boers and took possession of a spur and the southern summit. Soon afterwards the Rifle Brigade reached the same height. Both battalions then advanced to the summit. Further advance was halted by artillery fire from Brakfontein and rifle fire from the east. Despite the heavy bombardment, the Boer defenders on Vaalkrans redoubled their efforts. They suffered heavy casualties of 29 killed and 24 wounded (one mortally) and six who were made prisoner. Their Pom-Pom was extricated at the last moment by Viljoen who barely avoided capture. Viljoen was later to recall:

All the trees were torn up and smashed by shells, great blocks of rock had been splintered and were stained yellow by the lyddite; mutilated bodies were lying everywhere – Briton and Boer side by side; for during the short time Vaalkrantz had been in their possession the English had not had an opportunity of burying the bodies of friend or foe.

The casualties sustained by the British exceeded those of the Boers on that day. Some 164 men were killed or wounded; the Durham Light Infantry had 87 casualties while the Rifle Brigade lost 77 men.

In the wake of the storming party there followed the two battalions (the 2nd Scottish Rfles and the 3rd King's Royal Rifles) of Lyttleton's Brigade. These movements were made under intense Boer fire. Their progress, under the river bank and into the mealie fields, was similar to the experience of the troops who advanced before them. Towards the close of day every effort was made to destroy the guns on the Boer left

Ben Viljoen Commandant of the Johannesburg Commando described the events of 5 February as follows, "I happened to be on the right flank with 95 burghers and a pom-pom...It seemed as if all the guns of the British army were being fired at us... On looking about me to see how my burghers were getting on I found that many around me had been killed and others were wounded... A lyddite shell suddenly burst over our heads. Four burghers beside me were blown to pieces and my rifle was smashed. It seemed to me as if a huge cauldron of boiling fat had burst over us and for some minutes I must have lost consciousness. A mouthful of brandy and water was given to me and restored me somewhat, and when I opened my eyes I saw the enemy climbing the koppie (knoll) on three sides of us, some of them only a hundred paces away." Viljoen and his men managed to escape, taking the pom-pom with them.

British infantrymen advance from Swartkop towards the pontoon bridge No. 4 (see map on page 40) for the attack on Vaalkrans on the afternoon of 6 February. Smoke caused by exploding shells can be seen on the slopes of Vaalkrans. The British fired 9 599 shells from 72 guns during the course of the battle from 5 to 7 February.

flank. The positions were eventually located, but the guns were only partially exposed when actually firing and recoiled behind the crest line after discharging their projectiles.

By 16:00 the British had seized the southern koppies of Vaalkrans. However, a brief occupation sufficed to arouse doubts in the minds of its captors of being able to complete the objective. Immediately northward, separated by a deep saddle, the northern koppie of Vaalkrans was observed to be lined with trenches occupied by the Johannesburg Commando. Though shells had set the grass ablaze, it was still strongly held. The rifle fire from there and from the heights near Kranskloof, occupied by the Soutpansberg and Standerton Commandos, was directed on the flank and reverse side of the British in possession of Vaalkrans. In addition, artillery from near the Twin Peaks, Brakfontein and Green Hill then shelled the hill. It was also observed that the narrow defile through which the road passed, was exposed to such fire. Moreover, a practicable

The 4th and 6th Brigades gathering near Swartkop before the advance over the Thukela River to Vaalkrans.

position for the placing of artillery on Vaalkrans, the ultimate purpose for the capture of the hill, could not to be found. The infantrymen on the hill deployed themselves as best they could along the rocky crest. Pom-Pom fire and a series of fusillades from Mauser rifles on to the hill prompted the infantrymen to construct sangars to provide shelter.

Boer counter-moves

Viljoen's superior, General Tobias Smuts, made urgent appeals for reinforcements but none arrived. Louis Botha, returning from Pretoria, arrived at Elandslaagte station at midday on 5 February. After meeting Joubert, who informed him of the latest developments on the upper Thukela, he departed for the front, arriving at Viljoen's and Smuts' laager encampment behind Green Hill during the morning of 6 Februaury. Botha was able to instill enthusiasm into the ranks of his men.

It was soon realized that a wedge had been driven into their line. The commandos and the artillery were accordingly drawn towards the salient. From the western flank came 100 men of the Heidelberg Commando, to be followed by an additional 320, and 145 from Lydenburg and Ermelo respectively, while 400 men arrived with Meyer from Colenso and went to the assistance of Smuts on the Boer eastern flank. 200 men from the Pretoria Commando laager and 50 of the Utrecht Commando arrived from Ladysmith. Two field guns were placed at the entrance of Doringkloof. Viljoen's Pom-Pom was moved to Green Hill, while a Krupp was moved to a position 2 700 metres north of Vaalkrans. On Doringkop a 155 mm Long Tom, brought from Ladysmith, was mounted in a shell-proof work. Thus by daybreak on the 6th the Boer left flank had received some additional 1 200 men and at least four guns (see map on page 40).

Buller believed that the value of Vaalkrans depended on the possibility of establishing artillery on the hill. The strength and proximity of the

A shell bursting in front of a Boer gun. (This is probably a staged photograph.)

The 1ˢᵗ Durham Light Infantry advancing on Vaalkrans.

Boers near Kranskloof, northern Vaalkrans and on Green Hill to the east, led Lyttelton to deploy his men along the rocky crest. The men, weary as they were from the day's fighting, began a long night's toil to protect themselves. Their discomfort was increased owing to the sudden outbursts of Pom-Pom shells and later Mauser fire at close quarters, creating the impression that a Boer capture of the hill was imminent.

The battle continues

Buller intended that both Kranskloof and northern Vaalkrans were to be shelled before the infantry could occupy them. On the morning of 6 February the battle was renewed with heavy exchanges of artillery: the Boer gunners concentrating on Vaalkrans and the British guns firing on to suspected Boer gun positions and Kranskloof. A Long Tom began firing early in the morning. It directed its fire at the British artillery pieces on Naval Gun Hill and Swartkop. A little later a shell from the 4.7 on Naval Gun Hill exploded within the works of the Long Tom. (Another account

A 5-inch gun shelling the Boer Long Tom on Doringkop. It was left to the gunners of a 4.7-inch naval gun positioned near Naval Gun Hill to score a direct hit on Long Tom's powder magazine and silence it.

says that the hit on the Boer gun came from a projectile fired from a 5-in army gun near Swartkop in conjunction with the 4.7.) There was a loud report and a column of smoke issued skywards. Viljoen maintained that the Boer artillerymen in charge of the Long Tom failed to place the gunpowder in a safe place and it was soon struck by a lyddite shell which set it ablaze. For several hours the gun remained silent whilst a fresh supply was obtained from the Main Laager near Ladysmith. By 06:40, in spite of the assistance of artillery, Lyttleton found it still impossible to attempt the seizure of northern Vaalkrans. He requested that No. 2 pontoon be removed and assembled at a spot close under Vaalkrans in order to make a retreat easier should it be necessary to abandon the hill.

Asked by Buller if there was any chance of an attack by an infantry brigade west of Vaalkrans, Lyttleton replied in the negative, saying that Kranskloof was still firmly held, but adding that an advance past the east of Vaalkrans was a better prospect. Buller requested Lyttelton to hold onto Vaalkrans until relieved at sundown, while he (Buller) would "await developments". Lyttelton added that the boulder terrain of Vaalkrans made it impossible for the mounting of artillery. Buller estimated that to force back the Boer lines would incur 2 000 to 3 000 casualties. He cabled these views to the Commander in Chief, Lord Roberts (who had replaced Buller), of whom he enquired whether he thought the relief of Ladysmith was worth the risk. Roberts replied that he was in favour of perseverance, and to the troops that the honour of the British Empire was in their hands and that his confidence was in their ultimate success.

There was scarcely any change on either side as the day wore on. The shellfire neither ceased nor decreased. Vaalkrans continued to be the focus of the Boer bombardment, although occasional shells from the Long Tom fell among the British troops there or on the batteries on the plain or shattered trees on Swartkop. By midday Botha realized that the capture of Vaalkrans was not possible, stating that the British troops were protected to their rearward by the Thukela, whilst an attack across the

The Johannesburg Commando.

open ground from the east would be foolhardy. Accordingly, he ordered the artillery to bombard the British positions on Vaalkrans. Shortly after 15:00 the Boer riflemen on northern Vaalkrans opened up a hot fire from behind burning grass. The attack, lasting less than 30 minutes, was beaten back after which the Boers maintained a constant discharge from their rifles at a distance, supported by artillery.

Towards evening the No. 2 pontoon bridge had been assembled under Vaalkrans (shown as No. 4 on map on page 40) and Hildyard's (2nd) Brigade crossed the river and relieved the 4th Brigade after their 26 hours occupation. Lyttleton reported to Buller, who at the time was having dinner and enquired as to the activities of the 4th Brigade. Lyttelton replied "Very bad; shot at day and night from nearly all sides by an invisible foe, against whom our fire was perfectly innocuous".

"Wait a bit," replied Buller who returned from his tent with some champagne. Lyttelton remarked that it was the most refreshing drink he ever had.

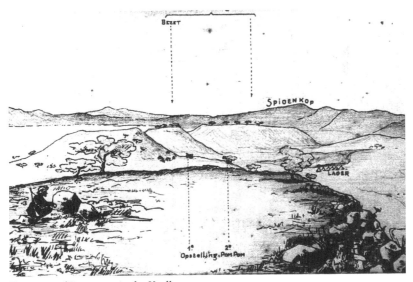

Positions of Boer guns in the Vaalkrans area.

On Vaalkrans, the 2nd Royal West Surrey replaced the Durham Light infantry to the north-west, the 2nd East Surrey prolonging the line, whilst the 2nd West Yorkshires manned the sangars (low fortifications) of the Rifle Brigade on the southern shoulder of the hill. The Devonshires, having being relieved by the 1st Connaught Rangers of Hart's (5th) Brigade, took post behind the southern koppie of Vaalkrans (see map on page 40). A spasmodic shellfire did not cease with the fall of darkness and harassed the relief. Thereupon the fresh troops set themselves to improve the defences. They, too, were disturbed by rifle fire directed at them from close quarters.

The next day (7 February) was also ushered in by a further artillery duel. The Boer guns, paying less attention to the British batteries, concentrated their fire upon Vaalkrans. The new occupants, sheltering behind strong sangars, were afforded fair cover, though a few losses occurred. Nevertheless the soldiers were pinned to their shelters; the heat

Typical fortifications the Boers had on the heights overlooking the Thukela valley. Many of the Boer fortifications on the upper Thukela remain well preserved.

A Long Tom (155mm Creusot) gun passing through the Sunday's River. One of these guns was in use on Doringkop.

was intense and food and water were only obtained at the risk of life. The northern koppie of Vaalkrans and the high ground near Kranskloof, still strongly held by the Boers, proved an annoying feature. Hildyard made a personal reconnaissance of it. If seized, its tenure would be doubtful, its fortification difficult and both flanks could easily be enfiladed by Boers.

Throughout the action the Boer guns shelled Vaalkrans, Swartkop, the pontoons and the river loop in which were concentrated some infantry units. The British guns, at times fruitlessly searching for the Boer guns, expended approximately 9 600 shells during the three days; this was considered the heaviest bombardment of the entire Anglo-Boer War.

The British retire

At 16:00 Buller called together his generals. After hearing various suggestions, he announced his intention of abandoning his present attempt and of seeking a more viable position from which to pierce the Boer line.

Confronted with a report that an army of 16 000 men was barring the advance to Ladysmith, he considered the persistence on Vaalkrans hill a useless waste of life. At 17:45 he issued orders for withdrawal.

Meanwhile the artillery fire on both sides never slackened, the bombardment of Vaalkrans increasing in severity in the late afternoon. At nightfall it ceased and the British troops, emerging from their shelters for the first time, prepared for a retreat. The evacuation, made quietly, did not arouse the Boer riflemen nearby. By 21:00, leaving a token force on Vaalkrans, the remainder of the infantrymen descended the rocky hillside and crossed the Thukela by No. 4 pontoon at its foot. At this moment the Boers opened a heavy fire against the top of Vaalkrans, to which the thin line of remaining troops replied vigorously for 15 minutes. Soon after 22:00 these troops also left the hill and crossed the river. The pontoons of No. 4 bridge were rapidly drawn ashore and packed and by midnight no British soldier remained on the left bank of the Thukela.

The British casualties, particularly of the infantry from Vaalkrans, were brought by a steady stream of stretcher bearers to a field hospital below the north-western spur of Swartkop. The cases were sorted according to the degree of severity of their wounds. The most severe cases were relieved of pain by injection of morphia. Others, who required immediate surgical attention, were sent to a special marquee for this purpose. The not-so-serious were removed on stretchers or ambulances to the No. 4 Stationary Hospital at Spearman's farm. The field hospital did not escape from its share of projectiles. Several shells from Long Tom landed close to the hospital, one of which exploded some 10 metres from the operating tent causing no injury, while two others landing nearby failed to explode.

Early on 8 February the Boers, discovering that Vaalkrans was abandoned, found the corpses of Boers and five British soldiers. In addition seven Boers, who were wounded three days previously, were discovered, one of whom subsequently died. Several British graves were found. (A year later two skeletons found on the battlefield were buried.) meanwhile the Boer gunners on Doringkop were engaging in an artillery duel with the British Naval 4.7-inch gun. A shell from Long Tom exploded to the rear of the Dublin Fusiliers, killing one soldier. By 08:00 the head of the column was ascending the heights at the foot of Mt Alice while the rear still lingered on the track past Harding's farm. The 5th Infantry Brigade followed the main body to Springfield where it went into bivouac at 16:30.

There still remained the evacuation of the force occupying the Maconochie Koppies and the removal of the No. 1 pontoon at Potgieter's Drift. Bringing the artillery down along the steep slopes of Swartkop and under Naval Gun Hill proved almost more toilsome and dangerous than previously during its ascent. The stores from Spearman's farm were sent to Springfield and then onto Chieveley. These tasks, which required the use of 559 wagon loads, were completed in 17 hours on 9 February.

Conclusion and casualties

Thus ended the fourth British attempt to relieve the beleaguered town of Ladysmith. Although the feint attack towards Brakfontein was carried out with admirable precision, it proved futile in view of the course of subsequent events. The Boers remained in the positions on Brakfontein. The exposure of a few regiments on Vaalkrans hill to the concentration of the Boers' guns and rifles without a rapid follow-up by the British men and guns, resulted in little chance of breaking through the Boer defences. Furthermore, Vaalkrans proved impracticable for the deployment of artillery. However, the commitment of more troops to capture the northern hill of Vaalkrans and Kranskloof beyond it might have succeeded on the first day. During the next two days the operation could have achieved success but at the cost of heavy casualties. Buller, ever mindful of incurring a high number of casualties amongst his men, and aware that the Boers were barring his way to Ladysmith, it was thought in great numbers, decided to abandon the Vaalkrans theatre. Two days later most of the Natal Field Force was at Chieveley and found itself once more opposite the heights at Colenso.

The Boer casualties were

Killed	38
Wounded	45
Missing in action	4
Total	**87**

The number of casualties sustained by the British are given by various primary sources, none of which concur. It is the opinion of the writer that the information as given in *The Times History of the War in South Africa* is the most accurate, namely

	Officers	Men
Killed or died of wounds	3	31
Wounded	17	318
Total	**20**	**349**

A detachment under Colonel JF Burn-Murdoch remained at Springfield to guard the British left flank. This was a mixed force of 2 800 men and eight guns. It was to remain for two weeks before joining the Natal Field Force on the Thukela Heights.

On 11 February, when most of the Natal Field Force was back at Chieveley, Botha, with detachments of several commandos, crossed the Thukela River at Munger's Drift.

They became engaged in a skirmish near Swartkop with some of the British cavalry during which the latter suffered five wounded and seven were captured. One of the captives was released in order to summon medical assistance while Botha and his party retired across the Thukela.

Forces engaged

BOER

East flank: Doringkloof, Vaalkrans, Commanding: Combat General T Smuts

Johannesburg, Standerton and Soutpansberg Commandos

Artillery: Two 75 mm Creusot guns, two Free State 75mm Krupps, one (perhaps two) Maxim-Nordenfeldts (Pom-Poms), one 155mm Creusot (Long Tom)

Total: 850 men

Centre: Brakfontein to Drielingkoppe (Twin Peaks). Commanding: Chief Commandant M Prinsloo

Senekal, Vrede, Winburg and Harrismith Commandos

Artillery: Two 75mm Krupps, two 75mm Creusots, one Pom-Pom, one 75mm Free State Krupp

Total: 940 men

West flank: Drielingkoppe to iNtabamnyama. Commanding: General SW Burger

Rustenburg, Lydenburg, Carolina, Heidelberg, Heilbron, Ermelo Commandos

There was also a German unit

Total: 1 780 to 1 830 men

Artillery not specified in the sources

BRITISH

Naval Brigade

Two 4.7-in guns, eight Naval 12-pdr

Total: 233 men

Mounted Troops

Six 15-pdr guns; three machine guns

1st Cavalry Brigade. Commanding Col JF Burn Murdoch

Royal Dragoons

13th Hussars

14th Hussars

'A' Battery Royal Horse Artillery

2nd Cavalry Brigade. Commanding Col Lord Dundonald

South African Light Horse

Thorneycroft's Mounted Infantry

Bethune's Mounted Infantry

Imperial Light Horse (1 squadron)

Natal Carbineers (1 squadron)

Natal Mounted Police (a detachment)

King's Royal Rifles (1 section)

Total: 2 753 men

Royal Artillery

Two 5-inch guns

Seven field batteries: 7th, 19th, 28th, 63rd, 73rd, 78th batteries

Royal Field Artillery (15 pounders) & 61st battery (howitzer)

Royal Garrison Artillery: No.4 Mountain Battery

Total: 1 879 men

Infantry

2nd Brigade, Commanding: Major-General HJT Hildyard

2nd Royal West Surrey Regiment

2nd Devonshire Regiment

2nd West Yorkshire Regiment

2nd East Surrey Regiment

4th Brigade

Commanding: Major-General NG Lyttelton

2nd Scottish Rifles

3rd King's Royal Rifle Corps

1st Durham Light Infantry

1st Rifle Brigade

11th Brigade

Commanding: Major-General AS Wynne

2nd Royal Lancaster Regiment

2nd Lancashire Fusiliers

1st South Lancashire Regiment

1st York and Lancaster Regiment

5th Brigade

1st Connaught Rangers

Total: 15 021 men

The terrain today

Vaalkrans Hill is located near Skietsdrift on the Thukela River over which the historic Voortrekker Wenkommando passed en route to do battle with the Zulus at Blood River on 16 December 1838.

The mortal remains of the British soldiers, whose graves were on the left bank of the Thukela and on Vaalkrans, have been exhumed and reinterred near the foot of the hill in the Vaalkrans Garden of Remembrance. The Garden contains a large British monument on which is inscribed the names of those who were killed in action or died of wounds and who were buried at Vaalkrans, Mount Alice farm (called Spearman's farm in 1900) and at Mooi River. In addition there is a memorial to Major Johnson-Smyth brought in from the bank of the Thukela River.

On the Burgher memorial in Ladysmith there is a list of 39 Boers who fell at Vaalkrans. Of the Boers found buried on the battlefield, the graves of eight were exhumed and their remains were transferred to the burgher monument. The graves of 31 men, belonging to the Johannesburg, Krugersdorp and Standerton Commandos, have to date not been located.

Under the slope of Swartkop where the British hauled up fourteen guns, there is evidence of the slide constructed for the purpose. After much searching the author located the site. On top of Swartkop nothing remains except a stone wall erected at the eastern end of the hill. Presumably this was built in order to protect the British ordnance from shell-fire, particularly from the Long Tom.

On Vaalkrans and Kranskloof are several well-preserved stone walls and gun emplacements built by the Boers and British soldiers.

Co-ordinates:
Swartkop: S28° 42.177' E29° 36.263'
Vaalkrans (centre of both features): S28° 40.604' E29° 37.297'
Vaalkrans Garden of Remembrance: S28° 40.519' E29° 37.851'
Potgieter's Drift: S28° 41.205' E29° 36.263'
Maconochie Koppies: S28° 40.808' E29° 34.552'
Brakfontein Ridge: S28° 38.393' E29° 34.680'

The battle: account by a private

Private Frederick Tucker was with the Rifle Brigade and fought in the battle of Vallkrans. Excerpts from his diary provide another perspective of the battle:

On 9 October, 1899, I received notice to rejoin the colours of the 1st Class Army Reserve. On 14 October I proceeded to Gosport and gave my papers in at the Rifle Depot, meeting several old comrades. Everything seemed strange to me but I soon felt at home once again.

15 October 1899

Passed by the Medical Officer and immediately after drew my kit and equipment. In the afternoon about fifty of us proceeded to Fort Brockhurst.

16 October 1899

In the morning did four hours aiming drill and then in the afternoon went to Brown down and commenced a short course of musketry.

After firing, marched back to Fort Brockhurst.

28 October 1899

About 8:30 a.m. we boarded two steamers and crossed over to Southampton, the cheers were magnificent as we left Cowes. On arrival at Southampton we embarked on the S.S. German of the Union Line. The Duke of Connaught, Lord Bingham and several ex-officers of the Rifle Brigade were there and inspected the Battalion. There was an immense number of people on the jetty. A cornet player made the scene more cheerful by playing lively airs and patriotic songs such as : 'Soldiers of the Queen' and 'Au Revoir'. At 2.00 p.m. we were towed out, everyone cheering like mad, both on the ship and on the pier. And so for the second time I leave the shores of Old England. I can only say ours was a grand send off: a very pretty and touching scene.

It was a very good voyage out, the food supplied to us was much better than that supplied to troops on ordinary troop ships and there was singing and dancing which was greatly enjoyed by both the troops and the passengers.

[Details of this period omitted.]

3 February 1900

We bivouacked at the foot of Spearman's Hill. Sunday, as well.

5 February 1900

Battle of Vaal Krantz

We fell in at 6.30 a.m. knowing we were to attack yet another of those hills which the Boers know how to fortify so well. With the Durham Light Infantry, we formed the firing line supported by the other two regiments of our brigade. We marched for about three miles under Spearman's Hill and then halted for some time to allow the Engineers time to build a pontoon bridge for the crossing of the Tugela. Meanwhile, our guns kept up a heavy fire, and it was a treat to watch our artillery, who took up position on the open plain, fully exposed to the enemy's long range guns which throw one hundred pound shells compared to our artillery 15-pound shells. Theirs carry 10 000 yards and ours 5 000 but nevertheless, our gunners kept up a brave fire. They could not reach the Boer Long Toms so they treated them with contempt and turned their fire instead on the Boer trenches. We could see that the attack was developing on the left front of us. The brigade who relieved us on Mount Alice were, with the aid of several battalions of artillery, making a false attack and had succeeded in drawing the Boer fire with their diversion. However, pom-pom, Mauser and big guns forced them to retire to a safer distance. The Engineers had succeeded in laying the bridge despite the heavy fire they were under and the stretchers were bringing back their wounded as we advanced. The Durhams led, crossing the bridge amidst a hail of Mauser and Maxim bullets – the Boers were firing for all they were worth. The first man of my regiment to step on the bridge was shot dead – hit in the head and the heart. We crossed over in single file at the double but even with this precaution several of our men were badly hit. Some excellent sprinting was done through air alive with bullets, like bees humming around. We formed up under the river bank, there were a lot of wounded men and the doctor was very busy. Almost immediately we left the bank of the river and found ourselves in a mealie field, where the Boers made it very lively for us with their big guns, rifle and pom-pom fire. (The men of my regiment have nick-named these mealie fields 'death-traps' as we are such exposed targets for the Boers as we pass through them.)

My regiment and the Durhams were still advancing in skirmishing order, no shot or shell could stop us that day and soon the foot of Vaal Krantz was reached, and, with fixed swords, we charged up the hill in the face of deadly shot and shell fire. When we reached the top we found only a few Boers remaining and these we took as prisoners. Very soon the whole of the regiment was on the hill and the men set to work at once building walls for protection as we were still under a very heavy cross fire from the front and the right. It was fortunate that we did this for as soon as our heads were shown above the wall a well-aimed volley rang out. The Boers kept firing until it was quite dark, so it was not safe to move our casualties, which were very heavy – about 80 in the Rifle Brigade. A few Boers kept sniping all night while we strengthened our walls.

At daybreak the Boers let us have it from all sides with their long range guns. Spion Kop sent us greetings with shells, and Groblers Kloof with its 8-inch gun, which came across with a noise like a traction engine. Their pom-poms, too, were very active and taken altogether we were having a very lively time, lying on the side of the bare hill (Vaal Krantz) with no one able to come to our assistance. The remainder of our troops were trapped on the other side of the river, unable to cross the open plain which lay between us because of the heavy Boer shell fire. We couldn't advance and wouldn't retire, so there we lay, as close to the ground as possible. We could not see a single Boer to aim at, only a trench about 1 000 yards in front of us which some of our men fired at just for the sake of something to do.

A great many men were wounded during the day while we waited, fully expecting some movement from the other troops, but none came. Twice the balloon went up and we were relieved at 7.00 p.m. under cover of darkness by another brigade led by Colonel Kitchener of the West Yorks who told Colonel Billy Norcott that we had been greatly praised by General Buller for the way we had taken the hill. The Boers made one attempt to retake it but they were driven back in such a hurry that they left one hundred rifles and several dead and wounded behind them; they did not try that game again!

Having been relieved, we marched back under Spearman's Hill again to bivouack for the night. I was not sorry to be away from the incessant noise of shot and shell – we had been under fire for thirty hours. It goes without saying that I slept soundly that night despite being on the open veldt without any covers. I woke early next morning, cold, stiff and shivering, my clothes wet through with the heavy dew. We lay on the side of Spearman's Hill all day waiting for the order to attack the remainder of the Boer positions and, occasionally, getting a shell close to us. No orders came to advance, indeed, the balloon appeared to be the only thing at work with the exception of the guns! Night fell and we bivouacked. During the night the bridges were taken up (another pontoon bridge had been placed close by Vaal Krantz), and the hill which we had lost so many lives taking was evacuated. So all our hopes of relieving Ladysmith this way were scattered.

I shall never forget our retirement: the Boers tried to hurry us up with the huge shells from their 8-inch Long Tom. We passed Generals Buller, Clery and Lyttelton; Clery was on a stretcher and looked very sick, while Buller had disappointment written all over his face. 'Come on, Rifle Brigade, hurry up!' he said, as we passed him, for we were not hurrying very much, we were reluctant to leave what we had won. I think my regiment was the last to leave, for when we passed Spearman's Hill, we found nearly all our division had marched off. The 4th Brigade, we learned, were to march to Chieveley.

After marching for some time we camped in Springfield. This was the first time we had been under canvas since leaving Frere on 10 January and it was a welcome change from sleeping in the open. Some of us had such luxuries as Quaker Oats, tins of cocoa, etc. stowed away in tent bags and we were soon busy making fires and cooking, each his own little mess tin full of whatever he possessed. Speaking for myself, I thoroughly enjoyed a meal of Quaker Oats followed by a good sleep without the expectation of being woken by a sudden alarm or a screaming shell.

On the following day we rested, passing the day bathing and washing our underclothing – a thing they were very much in need of!

10 February 1900

We struck camp. And marched seven miles towards Chieveley. That night we bivouacked on the open veldt again for a few hours sleep and early next morning we finished our march to Chieveley. ('A' Company on outpost.)

(Extract taken from P Todd & D Fordham, Private Tucker's Boer War Diary*, Elm Tree Books, London, 1980.)*

Additional reading

Amery, L.S. *The Times History of the War in South Africa* Vol III (London, Sampson Low, Marston and Company, 1905).

Breytenbach, J.H. *Die Geskiedenis van die Tweede Vryheidsoorlog in Suid Afrika* Vol III (Pretoria, Die Staatsdrukker, 1969–1978).

Crowe, G. *The Commission of HMS Terrible* (London, Newnes, 1903).

Maurice, F. and Grant, M.H. *History of the War in South Africa* Vol. II (London, Hurst and Blackett, 1907).

Pakenham, Thomas. *The Boer War* (Johannesburg, Jonathan Ball, 1979).

Viljoen, B. *My Reminiscences of the Anglo-Boer War* (Cape Town, Struik, 1903).

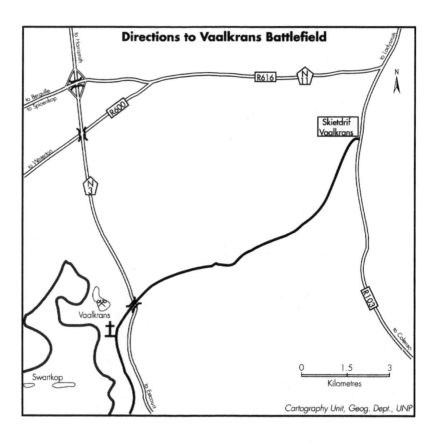

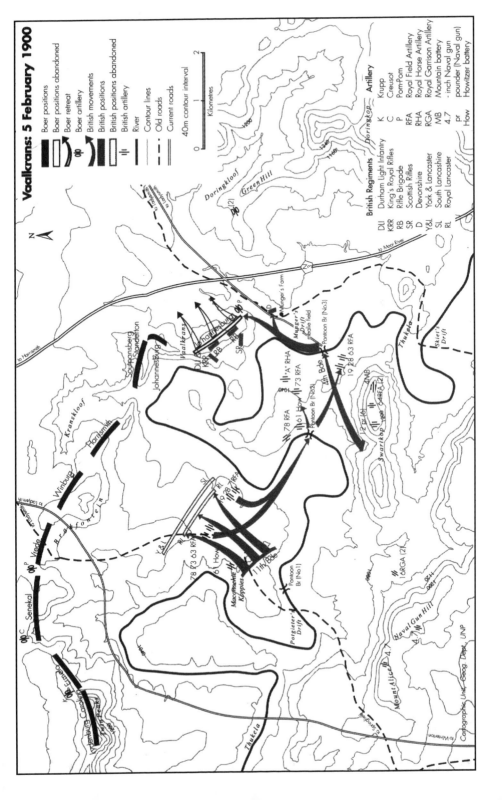

Vaalkrans: 5 February 1900

Boer positions
Boer positions abandoned
Boer retreat
Boer artillery
British movements
British positions
British positions abandoned
British artillery
River
Contour lines
Old roads
Current roads

40m contour interval

0 Kilometres 2

British Regiments

DLI	Durham Light Infantry
KRR	King's Royal Rifles
RB	Rifle Brigade
SR	Scottish Rifles
D	Devonshire
Y&L	York & Lancashire
SL	South Lancashire
Rl	Royal Lancaster

Artillery

K	Krupp
C	Creusot
P	PomPom
RFA	Royal Field Artillery
RHA	Royal Horse Artillery
RGA	Royal Garrison Artillery
MB	Mountain battery
4.7	- inch Naval gun
pr	pounder (Naval gun)
How	Howitzer battery

Doringkop

Cartographic Unit, Geog. Dept., UNP

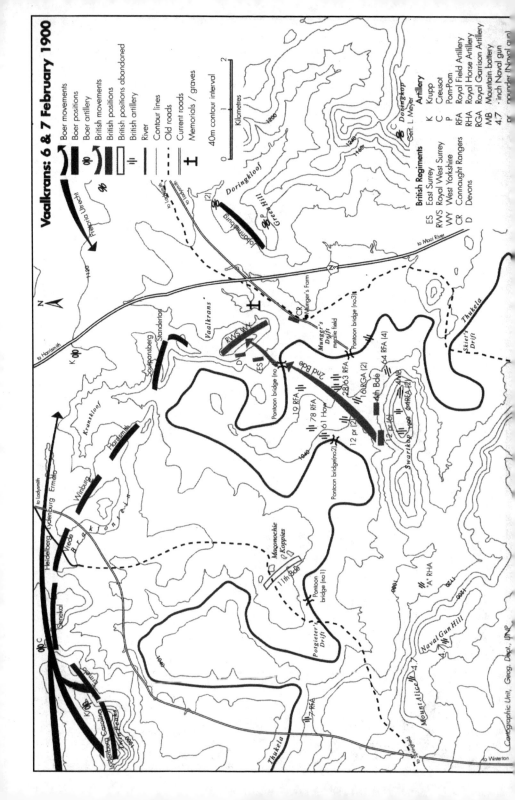

Vaalkrans: 6 & 7 February 1900

Legend:

- Boer movements
- Boer positions
- Boer artillery
- British movements
- British positions
- British positions abandoned
- British artillery
- River
- Contour lines
- Old roads
- Current roads
- Memorials / graves
- 40m contour interval

Kilometres 0 1 2

British Regiments
- ES — East Surrey
- RWS — Royal West Surrey
- WY — West Yorkshire
- CR — Connaught Rangers
- D — Devons

Artillery
- K — Krupp
- C — Creusot
- P — Pom-Pom
- RFA — Royal Field Artillery
- RHA — Royal Horse Artillery
- RGA — Royal Garrison Artillery
- MB — Mountain battery
- 4.7 - inch Naval gun
- or - pounder (Naval gun)

Cartographic Unit, Geog. Dept., UNP